Fermentation for Beginners

A Complete Step-by-Step Guide with 25 Recipes

Table of Contents

Introduction

When it comes to preserving food, there are several methods to choose from. Many people enjoy canning fresh foods to enjoy them later – plus, canning is a great way to save money! Another food preservation method that has become increasingly popular is fermentation. Not only can fermentation prepare foods for long-term storage, but it actually increases the nutritional value of the foods. By fermenting certain foods you can increase their vitamin and mineral content, increase the enzyme content to support healthy digestion, and neutralize anti-nutrients. Best of all, it is easy to do!

If you have ever thought about giving fermentation a try, this book is the perfect place for you to begin. Within the pages of this book you will receive an introduction to fermentation as well as an overview of the benefits associated with this type of food preservation. You will find a step-by-step guide for fermenting foods as well as a collection of 25 delicious recipes. If you are ready to give fermentation a try, pick a recipe and get going!

Fermentation Step-by-Step Guide

The process of fermentation is fairly simple to understand. It is a process that takes place in the absence of oxygen with the help of beneficial microorganisms like yeast, mold, and bacteria. During fermentation, these beneficial microorganisms break down the starches and sugars present in the food ingredients, transforming them into acids and alcohols. In doing so, the nutritional content of the food actually increases and it can be stored for a longer period of time without risk of spoiling.

There are three different types of fermentation – lacto-fermentation, ethyl alcohol fermentation, and acetic fermentation. Lacto-fermentation is facilitated by yeasts and bacteria which convert sugars and starches into lactic acid – lactic acid helps with pre-digestion, pancreatic function, and blood circulation. Ethyl alcohol fermentation is facilitated by beneficial microorganisms that convert carbohydrates into alcohol. Acetic fermentation occurs when alcohol is exposed to air and is then converted into acetic acid, or vinegar.

The key to fermentation is to create and maintain a specific environment so the microorganisms can do their work. The environment needs to be free from spoiling organisms and maintained at the right temperature – you also have to make sure the right sugars and starches are available for the microorganisms. Some foods can take a few days to ferment properly while others might take weeks or months. You can speed up the fermentation process by using brine (a salt and water combination) and a starter culture like whey.

You will find a recipe for both of these below:

Basic Brine Recipe

Every recipe is different but, for the most part, you will only use this basic brine in lacto-fermented vegetable recipes. When fermenting vegetables you will be compacting the ingredients into the jar, pounding them down until they release their natural juices. If the natural juices are not sufficient to cover the mixture in the jar you can add some of this brine – just be sure to leave the recommended amount of headspace at the top.

- 6 tablespoons fine sea salt
- 8 cups filtered water

1. Combine the salt and water in a large jar and stir it until the salt is dissolved.
2. Use the recommended amount of brine as called for in the recipe.

Basic Whey Recipe

Many people prefer to use salt when fermenting food – especially vegetables – but whey is another viable option. When you use whey as your starter culture just keep in mind that it will impact the flavor of your recipe. You can also choose to use a small amount of whey in combination with the salt brine to add flavor and to keep vegetables crunchy.

- 2 cups play organic yogurt

1. Spoon the yogurt into a cheesecloth and tie up to edges into a bundle.
2. Hang the bag over a glass or bowl to collect the drippings.
3. Let the bag drip for 24 hours until you've collected about 1 cup of whey.
4. Transfer the whey to a jar and store it in the refrigerator until ready to use.

Now that you know the basics about what fermentation is and how it works you are ready to learn the process. The fermentation process is fairly simple to get started, you just have to combine the right materials and then wait. Below you will find a step-by-step guide as an example of the fermentation process:

1. Prepare your ingredients for fermentation – this may mean chopping, slicing, grating, or shredded, depending on the recipe.

2. Decide whether you will be using a brine, a whey, or another starter culture – refer to the recipe for instructions.
3. Prepare your brine according to the instructions provided earlier.
4. Place your ingredients in a jar and pour in the brine – you may need to use something to weigh down the ingredients to keep them submerged.
5. Give the ingredients time to ferment – refer to the instructions in the recipe for the proper length of time.
6. Transfer the fermented food to cold storage until you are ready to enjoy them.

By following the basic step-by-step guide above you can ferment all kinds of different foods. If you are ready to get started, turn to the next page then pick a recipe and give it a try!

Fermentation Recipes

Recipes Included in this Book:

Lacto-Fermented Mayonnaise

Lacto-Fermented Hot Sauce

Lacto-Fermented Ketchup

Lacto-Fermented Salsa

Lacto-Fermented Peach Chutney

Lacto-Fermented Carrots and Onions

Lacto-Fermented Turnips

Lacto-Fermented Broccoli Cauliflower Blend

Lacto-Fermented Parsnips

Lacto-Fermented Carrot-Apple Blend

Easy Sauerkraut

Spicy Kimchi

Garlic Dill Pickles

Homemade Horseradish

Beetroot Relish

Homemade Yogurt

Matsoni

Coconut Yogurt

Fermented Lemonade

Kombucha

Fermented Orange Juice

Beet Kvass

Fermented Raspberry Lemonade

Milk Kefir

Kefir Iced Tea

Lacto-Fermented Mayonnaise

Ingredients:

- 6 large egg yolks, whisked well
- 3 tablespoons fresh lemon juice
- 2 tablespoons whey
- 2 teaspoons Dijon mustard
- 1 teaspoon sea salt
- 2 cups olive oil

Instructions:

1. Let all of the ingredients rest until they reach room temperature.
2. Combine all but the olive oil in a food processor and blend smooth.
3. With the processor running, drizzle in the olive oil.
4. Spoon the mixture into a jar, leaving 1 inch of headspace at the top.
5. Let rest at room temperature for 8 to 12 hours.
6. Transfer to the refrigerator and store for up to 2 months.

Lacto-Fermented Hot Sauce

Ingredients:

- 10 cayenne peppers, chopped
- 1 small yellow onion, diced
- 1 tablespoon fresh minced garlic
- 2 cups filtered water
- 1 ½ tablespoons sea salt

Instructions:

1. Combine the peppers, onions, and garlic in a glass jar.
2. Whisk together the water and salt until the salt is dissolved.
3. Pour the brine into the jar until the ingredients are covered then cover the jar with a book or plate to keep the vegetables submerged.
4. Let the jar sit for 1 to 3 weeks until fermented.
5. Strain the ingredients, reserving ½ cup of liquid, and place them in a food processor.
6. Blend with up to ½ cup of the reserved liquid until the sauce is smooth.
7. Pour the sauce into a jar and store in the refrigerator for up to 2 months.

Lacto-Fermented Ketchup

Ingredients:

- 2 (6-ounce) cans tomato paste
- 1/3 cup raw honey
- ¼ cup plus 1 tablespoon filtered water
- 2 tablespoons apple cider vinegar
- 2 tablespoons whey
- ¾ teaspoon sea salt
- ¼ teaspoon ground cinnamon
- Pinch dry mustard powder
- Pinch ground cloves
- Pinch allspice

Instructions:

1. Combine all of the ingredients in a food processor and blend smooth.
2. Transfer the mixture to a jar, leaving 1 inch of headspace at the top.
3. Cover the jar and let rest at room temperature for 2 days.
4. Transfer the jar to the refrigerator and store for up to 2 months.

Lacto-Fermented Salsa

Ingredients:

- 24 large tomatoes, chopped
- 2 large yellow onions, diced
- 2 cups jalapeno, chopped
- ¼ cup dried oregano
- 2 tablespoons ground cumin
- 2 tablespoons fresh minced garlic
- ¼ cup sea salt
- Saltwater brine, if needed

Instructions:

1. Combine all of the ingredients in a food processor and pulse until finely chopped.
2. Transfer the mixture to a jar, leaving 1 inch of headspace at the top.
3. Pound the ingredients down to compact and release the juices.
4. If the natural juices do not cover the mixture, add enough saltwater brine to do so.
5. Place something heavy on top of the jar to keep the ingredients submerged then let rest at room temperature for 3 to 5 days.
6. Transfer the jar to the refrigerator and store for up to 2 months.

Lacto-Fermented Peach Chutney

Ingredients:

- 8 ripe pears, peeled, cored and chopped
- 2 medium yellow onions, chopped
- 2 jalapenos, seeded and chopped
- 1 cup seedless raisins
- 1 cup chopped pecans
- 2 tablespoons fresh grated ginger
- ½ cup fresh lemon juice
- 1 ½ tablespoons sea salt
- Saltwater brine, if needed

Instructions:

1. Combine all of the ingredients in a food processor and pulse until finely chopped.
2. Transfer the mixture to a jar, leaving 1 inch of headspace at the top.
3. Pound the ingredients down to compact and release the juices.
4. If the natural juices do not cover the mixture, add enough saltwater brine to do so.
5. Place something heavy on top of the jar to keep the ingredients submerged then let rest at room temperature for 3 to 5 days.
6. Transfer the jar to the refrigerator and store for up to 2 months.

Lacto-Fermented Carrots and Onions

Ingredients:

- 4 cups sliced carrots
- 4 medium yellow onions, chopped
- 1 tablespoon fresh grated ginger
- 1 tablespoon fresh minced garlic
- 6 tablespoons sea salt
- Saltwater brine, if needed

Instructions:

1. Combine the carrots and onions in a food processor.
2. Pulse several times to combine then pulse in the ginger, garlic and salt.
3. Spoon the mixture into jars and pound the ingredients down to compact and release the juices – leave 1 inch of headspace at the top.
4. Add a small amount of saltwater brine, if needed, to cover the vegetables.
5. Weigh down the ingredients using a plate or weighted lid and cover with a clean towel.
6. Let the jar rest at room temperature for 3 to 5 days until fermented.
7. Transfer the jar to the refrigerator and store for up to 2 months.

Lacto-Fermented Turnips

Ingredients:

- 5 lbs. fresh turnips, peeled and cut into sticks
- 2 tablespoons sea salt
- Saltwater brine, if needed

Instructions:

1. Pack the turnips into a large glass jar, pounding them down while sprinkling with salt to release the juices.
2. Fill the jar to within 1 inch of the top, adding saltwater brine if needed to keep the vegetables submerged.
3. Weigh down the ingredients using a plate or weighted lid and cover with a clean towel.
4. Let the jar rest at room temperature for 7 to 10 days until fermented.
5. Transfer the jar to the refrigerator and store for up to 2 months.

Lacto-Fermented Broccoli Cauliflower Blend

Ingredients:

- 2 cups chopped cauliflower florets
- 2 cups chopped broccoli florets
- 2 large carrots, sliced thin
- 2 medium ripe apples, cored and chopped
- 2 ½ tablespoons fresh grated ginger
- ½ cup sea salt
- Saltwater brine, if needed

Instructions:

1. Combine the cauliflower, broccoli, carrots, and apples in a food processor.
2. Pulse several times to combine then pulse in the ginger and salt.
3. Spoon the mixture into jars and pound the ingredients down to compact and release the juices – leave 1 inch of headspace at the top, adding saltwater brine if needed to keep the vegetables submerged.
4. Weigh down the ingredients using a plate or weighted lid and cover with a clean towel.
5. Let the jar rest at room temperature for 3 to 5 days until fermented.
6. Transfer the jar to the refrigerator and store for up to 2 months.

Lacto-Fermented Parsnips

Ingredients:

- 5 lbs. fresh parsnips, peeled and cut into sticks
- 2 tablespoons sea salt
- Saltwater brine, if needed

Instructions:

1. Pack the turnips into a large glass jar, pounding them down while sprinkling with salt to release the juices.
2. Fill the jar to within 1 inch of the top, adding saltwater brine if needed to keep the vegetables submerged.
3. Weigh down the ingredients using a plate or weighted lid and cover with a clean towel.
4. Let the jar rest at room temperature for 7 to 10 days until fermented.
5. Transfer the jar to the refrigerator and store for up to 2 months.

Lacto-Fermented Carrot-Apple Blend

Ingredients:

- 4 cups sliced carrots
- 4 medium ripe apples, cored and chopped
- 1 bunch green onions, sliced thin
- 2 ½ tablespoons fresh grated ginger
- 6 to 8 tablespoons sea salt
- Saltwater brine, if needed

Instructions:

1. Combine the carrots, apples, and green onions in a food processor.
2. Pulse several times to combine then pulse in the ginger and salt.
3. Spoon the mixture into jars and pound the ingredients down to compact and release the juices – leave 1 inch of headspace at the top.
4. If the natural juices do not cover the mixture, add enough saltwater brine to do so.
5. Weigh down the ingredients using a plate or weighted lid and cover with a clean towel.
6. Let the jar rest at room temperature for 3 to 5 days until fermented.
7. Transfer the jar to the refrigerator and store for up to 2 months.

Easy Sauerkraut

Ingredients:

- 4 heads green cabbage, shredded or sliced thin
- ¼ cup sea salt
- Saltwater brine, if needed

Instructions:

1. Place the sauerkraut in a large glass jar and pound it down to release the juices while sprinkling with salt.
2. Leave 1 inch of headspace at the top and add saltwater brine, if needed, to make sure the ingredients are submerged.
3. Weigh down the ingredients using a plate or weighted lid and cover with a clean towel.
4. Let the jar rest at room temperature for 7 to 10 days until fermented.
5. Transfer the jar to the refrigerator and store for up to 2 months.

Spicy Kimchi

Ingredients:

- 2 heads Napa cabbage, sliced thin
- 2 radishes, peeled and sliced thin
- 5 large carrots, peeled and sliced
- 1 bunch green onions, sliced thin
- 1/3 to ½ cup chili paste
- ¼ cup fish sauce
- 1 ¼ cups sea salt
- 1 head garlic, peeled and chopped
- 2 tablespoons fresh grated ginger

Instructions:

1. Soak the cabbage in saltwater overnight then strain the mixture well.
2. Combine the cabbage with the remaining ingredients, tossing with the salt.
3. Pack the ingredients into a large glass jar, pounding on the ingredients to compact and release the juices – leave 1 inch of headspace at the top.
4. If the natural juices do not cover the mixture, add enough saltwater brine to do so.
5. Weigh down the ingredients using a plate or weighted lid and cover with a clean towel.
6. Let the jar rest at room temperature for 5 to 7 days until fermented.
7. Transfer the jar to the refrigerator and store for up to 2 months.

Garlic Dill Pickles

Ingredients:

- 16 cups small pickling cucumbers
- 2 bunches fresh dill, chopped
- 16 cloves garlic, peeled
- 3 tablespoons pickling spice
- 12 tablespoons sea salt, divided
- 8 cups filtered water

Instructions:

1. Soak the cucumbers in cold water and scrub them clean.
2. Pack the cucumbers, dill, garlic, and pickling spices into large glass jars, sprinkling with 5 tablespoons sea salt as you do.
3. Whisk together the rest of the salt and water until the salt is dissolved.
4. Pour the brine into the jars until the ingredients are covered then cover the jar.
5. Let the jar rest at room temperature for 5 to 10 days until fermented.
6. Transfer the jar to the refrigerator and store for up to 2 months.

Homemade Horseradish

Ingredients:

- 1 cup fresh horseradish, peeled and chopped
- 1 ½ teaspoons sea salt
- ¼ cup fresh whey
- 2 to 4 tablespoons filtered water

Instructions:

1. Combine the horseradish, salt and whey in a food processor.
2. Pulse several times until the mixture is finely chopped.
3. Add 2 to 4 tablespoons water and blend until it forms a smooth paste.
4. Spoon the mixture into jars, adding water if needed to fill – leave 1 inch of headspace at the top.
5. Cover the jars loosely with the lid and let the jars rest at room temperature for 3 to 7 days until fermented.
6. Transfer the jar to the refrigerator and store for up to 2 months.

Beetroot Relish

Ingredients:

- 1 ½ pounds fresh beets, peeled and chopped
- 1 lbs. cored apples, chopped
- 2 star anise pods
- 1 tablespoon whole cloves
- Up to 1 tablespoon sea salt
- Saltwater brine, if needed
- Vegetable starter culture, as needed

Instructions:

1. Combine the beets and apples in a food processor and pulse until finely shredded.
2. Transfer to a bowl and toss in the anise pods and cloves.
3. Spoon the mixture into jars, sprinkling with salt and starter culture, and pound the ingredients down to compact and release the juices.
4. If the natural juices do not cover the mixture, add enough saltwater brine to do so.
5. Weigh down the ingredients using a plate or weighted lid and cover with a clean towel.
6. Let the jar rest at room temperature for 3 to 5 days until fermented then pour into a blender and blend smooth.
7. Pour the mixture back into the jar and store in the refrigerator and store for up to 2 months.

Homemade Yogurt

Ingredients:

- 4 cups whole milk
- ¼ cup mesophilic yogurt starter culture

Instructions:

1. Pour the milk into a saucepan and heat until just steaming – do not boil.
2. Transfer the milk to the refrigerator and chill for 30 minutes.
3. Whisk in your yogurt culture until smooth.
4. Pour the mixture into a large glass jar and cover with the lid.
5. Let the yogurt rest at room temperature for 24 hours or until it forms a clean break.
6. Store the finished yogurt in the refrigerator.

Matsoni

Ingredients:

- 4 cups whole milk
- ¼ cup matsoni starter culture

Instructions:

1. Whisk together the milk and matsoni starter culture in a large bowl.
2. Pour the mixture into a large glass jar and cover loosely with the lid.
3. Let the yogurt rest at room temperature for 1 to 2 days until it forms a clean break.
4. Store the finished yogurt in the refrigerator.

Coconut Yogurt

Ingredients:

- 8 cups coconut milk
- Starter yogurt culture
- 3 tablespoons gelatin
- 2 tablespoons raw honey
- 2 teaspoons vanilla extract

Instructions:

1. Pour the coconut milk into a saucepan and heat to 180°F then remove from heat and cool to 105°F.
2. Transfer the milk to a large glass jar, reserving 1 cup of it.
3. Whisk the starter culture into the reserved cup of milk.
4. Stir the milk mixture into the milk in the jar then place it in a yogurt maker.
5. Let the yogurt brew for 8 to 12 hours then remove from the yogurt maker.
6. Bring 2 tablespoons of water to boil in a small saucepan.
7. Whisk in the gelatin, honey and vanilla extract then whisk the mixture into the yogurt.
8. Divide the yogurt among glass jars then chill for 6 to 8 hours until it forms a clean break.
9. Blend the yogurt in a blender until smooth then store in the refrigerator.

Fermented Lemonade

Ingredients:

- 6 lemons, juiced
- ½ cup organic cane sugar
- ½ cup whey
- Filtered water, as needed

Instructions:

1. Whisk together the lemon juice, sugar and whey in a large glass jar.
2. Stir in the filtered water until the sugar dissolves.
3. Add enough water to fill the jar within 1 inch of the top then cover with a lid.
4. Cover the jar with a clean towel then let rest at room temperature for 2 days.
5. Transfer the jar to the refrigerator to store.

Kombucha

Ingredients:

- 15 cups filtered water
- 1 cup organic cane sugar
- 2 tablespoons loose-leaf tea
- 2 cups store-bought kombucha
- 1 scoby

Instructions:

1. Bring the water to boil in a medium saucepan then remove from heat.
2. Stir in the loose-leaf tea and sugar until the sugar is dissolved then cool to room temperature.
3. Strain the mixture into a large glass pitcher then stir in 12 cups of water.
4. Add in the prepared kombucha and pour the mixture into a large glass jar.
5. Add the scoby then cover the jar with cloth and let rest at room temperature for 7 to 10 days until it reaches the desired flavor
6. Pour the kombucha into glass bottles and chill before serving.

Fermented Orange Juice

Ingredients:

- 2 ½ cups fresh orange juice
- 2 tablespoons whey
- Pinch sea salt
- Filtered water, as needed

Instructions:

1. Whisk together the orange juice, whey, and salt then pour into a glass jar.
2. Add about 1 cup of filtered water or enough to fill the jar within 1 inch of the top.
3. Cover the jar tightly and shake then store at room temperature for 48 hours.
4. Transfer the jar to the refrigerator and chill before serving.

Beet Kvass

Ingredients:

- 6 medium beets, peeled and chopped
- 1/3 cup sea salt

Instructions:

1. Stir together the beets and salt then place them in a glass jar.
2. Add enough filtered water to cover the beets and stir until the salt is dissolved.
3. Cover the jar and let rest at room temperature for 2 days until fermented.
4. Transfer the jar to the refrigerator to store.

Fermented Raspberry Lemonade

Ingredients:

- 1 ½ cups filtered water
- 1 ½ cups fresh raspberries
- ½ cup raw honey
- 1 ½ cups fresh lemon juice
- 4 cups prepared kombucha

Instructions:

1. Combine the water, raspberries, and honey to a saucepan and simmer for 10 minutes until tender.
2. Transfer the mixture to a blender and add the lemon juice.
3. Blend the mixture until smooth then pour the mixture into a large glass pitcher.
4. Add the kombucha and stir well then serve immediately.

Water Kefir

Ingredients:

- 6 cups filtered water
- ¼ cup organic cane sugar
- ¼ cup water kefir grains
- 2 dried figs
- 1 ripe lemon, quartered

Instructions:

1. Bring the water to boil in a large saucepan then whisk in the sugar and stir until dissolved.
2. Remove from heat and cool the mixture to room temperature.
3. Pour the water kefir grains into a large jar then stir in the sugar water.
4. Add the lemon and figs then cover the jar with the lid.
5. Let the jar rest at room temperature for 2 to 3 days until fermented.
6. Strain the mixture into a pitcher, discarding the lemons and figs then chill before enjoying.

Kefir Iced Tea

Ingredients:

- 6 cups filtered water
- ¼ cup organic cane sugar
- ¼ cup water kefir grains
- 1 ripe lemon, quartered
- Handful fresh mint leaves
- Boiling water, as needed

Instructions:

1. Bring the water to boil in a large saucepan then whisk in the sugar and stir until dissolved.
2. Remove from heat and cool the mixture to room temperature.
3. Pour the water kefir grains into a large jar then stir in the sugar water.
4. Add the lemon then cover the jar with the lid.
5. Let the jar rest at room temperature for 2 to 3 days until fermented.
6. Place the mint in a bowl and pour the boiling water over it.
7. Let steep for at least 15 minutes then strain and cool to room temperature.
8. Mix 1 part mint tea with 1 part water kefir and serve chilled.

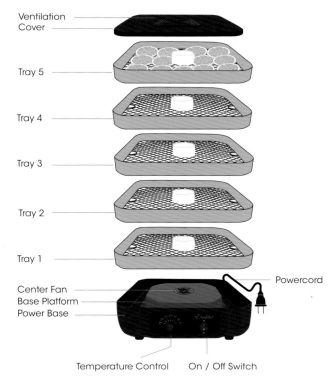

- Ventilation Cover
- Tray 5
- Tray 4
- Tray 3
- Tray 2
- Tray 1
- Center Fan
- Base Platform
- Power Base
- Powercord
- Temperature Control
- On / Off Switch

ACCESSORIES:
The following accessories are included with your dehydrator.

Plastic Tray Lining (5) Included

Yogurt Cups (4) Included

Drying Sheets (2) Included

Get To Know Your Excalibur:

GETTING STARTED

1. Remove cover and trays from base.
2. Uncoil cord from base.
3. Set base on a dry, level surface. Make sure there is enough space around the base and cover for sufficient airflow.
4. Food goes on the smooth side of the plastic tray lining. When drying stickier foods or liquid foods, we recommend placing a Paraflexx® dehydrator sheet or parchment paper on the plastic tray lining before loading food.
5. Once trays are loaded, place trays on the power base. Stack trays with the raised rib of the tray facing down.
6. Place cover on top stacked tray.
7. Plug cord into electrical outlet.
8. Set temperature.
9. Press ON and begin dehydrating.
10. Press OFF when dehydrating is complete.

CARE & CLEANING

1. Remove plug from wall outlet.
2. Remove trays from base.
3. Wash trays and plastic tray lining in warm water with a mild detergent or on top rack of dishwasher.
4. NOTE: Remove from dishwasher before drying cycle.
5. Wipe the dehydrator base with a soft, damp cloth. Do NOT dip or submerge the base in water or other liquid.

SAFETY FIRST

- For Household Use only.
- Do not place near a gas or electric burner.
- Do not place in a heated oven or microwave.
- Do not touch the hot surfaces.
- Do not let cord hang over edge of table or counter.
- Do not operate if cord or plug is damaged or after the appliance malfunctions. Call customer service for repair or adjustment.
- To protect against electrical shock, do not immerse power unit or any part of the cord and plug in water or other liquid.
- Unplug unit when not in use and before cleaning.
- Close supervision is necessary when appliance is used by or near children.
- Use of accessories or attachments not recommended by the manufacturer may cause injury.
- Do not use outdoors. Never block airflow to the bottom of the base. Never cover the entire unit. Never place on carpet, towel, newspaper, etc. Only place on a flat surface that provides sufficient airflow.
- Sharp utensils should not be used inside the dehydrator.
- Do not use this appliance for any reason other than its intended use.

Should you experience any problems with your dehydrator, contact technical support.

www.ExcaliburDehydrator.com

QUICKSTART TO DRYING:

Drying times may vary depending on food thickness, food water content, altitude, air humidity and temperature. If some food pieces dry faster than others, remove the dried food and place in an air tight container while the remaining food continues to dry.

FRUIT & VEGETABLES
- Wash fruits or vegetables
- Cut into small pieces (1/8" slices 1/4" rings)
- Add your ingredients
- Set your temperature best at (fruits) 135°F/57°C (vegetables) 125°F/52°C.
- Dehydration time can vary.

Our website and Preserve It Naturally! book have many recipes and "how-to's" on dehydrating fruits and vegetables in your dehydrator.

FRUIT LEATHERS & ROLL-UPS
- Select ripe or slightly overripe produce. Blend.
- Pour mix onto Paraflexx® or parchment paper on the plastic trays. Poured puree should be 1/4" to 1/8" thick.
- Set temperature at 135°F/57°C.
- Dry for 6-8 hours.
- Pureed strawberries and rhubarb, bananas and pineapples, bananas and peanut butter make great combinations.

JERKY
- Pick a lean cut of raw meat. The less fat, the better for jerky.
- Cut into uniform slices 1" wide and 3/8" thick.
- Marinate for 6-10 hours.
- Set temperature at 155°F/68°C. Dry for 6-8 hours. Dry beef, deer, bear, elk, chicken, turkey, fish and all your wild game.

HERBS & SPICES
- Trim off dead or discolored plant parts.
- Set temperature at 95°F/35°C – 115°F/46°C.
- Dry for 2-4 hours.

NUTS
- Soak nuts in cold water for 6-8 hours.
- Dry off with towel.
- Set dehydrator temperature at 115°F/46°C – 125°F/52°C.
- Dry for 10-14 hours.

RE-CRISPING
- Re-crisp stay crackers, chips, cookies or cereals.
- Place on drying trays,.
- Dry for 2 to 4 hours at 35°F/57°C.

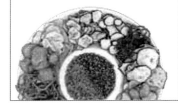

YOGURT
- Add 1 cup powdered milk to 1/2 gallon low-fat milk.
- Scald for 2 seconds. Remove from heat. Let cool.
- Add 2 tablespoons of non-pasteurized plain yogurt to cooled milk.
- Pour into containers and cover.
- Incubate in the dehydrator at 115°F/46°C or 5 hours.

CHEESE
Make soft cheeses, semi-soft and hard cheeses.

Our website and Preserve It Naturally! book have recipes and "how-to's" for fermenting cheese in your dehydrator.

MARINATE VEGETABLES
Marinating vegetables at a low temperature in a dehydrator, intensifies the flavor of food.

THICKEN SAUCES
Similar to the reduction technique.

- For 2 to 4 hours, place sauces in an open, glass container inside the dehydrator at a low temperature of 115°F/46°C.

WHOLE MEAL PREPARATION
Dehydrate whole meals that need only to be rehydrated.

Great for outdoor enthusiasts, hiking, camping, etc.

PET TREATS
Treat your pet to the best.

Our website and Preserve It Naturally! book have recipes and "how-to's" for making pet treats in your dehydrator.

POTPOURRI
- Simply place pedals on the plastic drying trays.
- Dry for 6-8 hours at 135°F/57°C.

Food	Time
Asparagus	5-6 hours
Beans	8-12 hours
Beets	8-12 hours
Broccoli	10-14 hours
Cabbage	7-11 hours
Carrots	6-10 hours
Celery	3-10 hours
Corn	6-10 hours
Cucumber	4-8 hours
Eggplant	4-8 hours
Greens	3-7 hours
Mushrooms	3-7 hours
Okra	4-8 hours
Onions	4-8 hours
Parsnips	7-11 hours
Peas	4-8 hours
Peppers	4-8 hours
Popcorn	4-8 hours
Potatoes	6-14 hours
Pumpkin	7-11 hours
Summer Squash	10-14 hours
Tomatoes	5-9 hours
Turnips	8-12 hours
Winter Squash	7-11 hours
Yams	7-11 hours
Zucchini	7-11 hours

Excalibur FOOD DEHYDRATOR.

8250 Fergusson Avenue, Sacramento, CA 95828
Phone: 916.381.4254 • Fax: 916.381.4256 | www.ExcaliburDehydrator.com

Conclusion

There are many different types of food preservation out there, and some of them are very complicated. Fortunately, fermentation is easy! By fermenting certain foods you can not only increase the nutritional value of the food, but you can also add to its shelf life. Fermenting foods does not require much special equipment or any rare materials – it is all about the preparation method you choose. If you are ready to give fermentation a try, this book may be just what you've been looking for. Not only have you received an introduction to fermentation and its benefits, but you have also been gifted with a collection of 25 delicious fermentation recipes. So what are you waiting for? Get cooking!

Made in the USA
Monee, IL
21 April 2022

95102262R00020